ADVENTURES IN COMPASSION

30 Acts of Love to Grow Heart and Soul.

Make Love Every Day

Rahbin Shyne

"Expand your definition of the word love and notice how big your heart becomes."
—Panache Desai

This book is dedicated to Earth, and all who honor her as home. As we expand our capacity to love one another, we expand our capacity to love and care for this marvelous place the human family calls home.

©2013 All Rights Reserved.
<u>Shyne@ShyneEveryDay.com</u>
P. O. Box, 90533, Long Beach, CA 90809

Contents

Compassion in Action 1
Day 1: Smile 5
Day 2: Compliment Someone You Know 7
Day 3 Smell The Flowers, Notice the Birds 9
Day 4 "You're Beautiful" 11
Day 5 Listen 13
Day 6 Clean Something 15
Day 7 Planet Earth 17
Day 8 Give Away One Dollar 19
Day 9 Express Thanks 22
Day 10 Compliment a Stranger 24
Day 11 Give Away Words 26
Day 12 Share A Talent 28
Day 13 Donate Something 30
Day 14 Express Gratitude 32
Day 15 Use Words Intentionally 34
Day 16 Love You 36
Day 17 Love Through Style 38
Day 18 Give 10 Minutes 40
Day 19 Say "I Love You." 42
Day 20 Make A List of Loves 44
Day 21 Share Food 46
Day 22 Touch of Love 49

DAY 23	DO SOMETHING FOR THE PLANET	51
DAY 24	MAKE A REQUEST	53
DAY 25	SHARE LAUGHTER	55
DAY 26	FORGIVE	57
DAY 27	GIVE SOMETHING AWAY	59
DAY 28	BE CURIOUS	62
DAY 29	LOVE AGAIN	64
DAY 30	REPEAT YOUR FAVORITE	66
DAY 31!	CONGRATULATIONS!	68

"A new command I give you: Love one another. As I have loved you, so you must love one another."
–Jesus of Nazareth

COMPASSION IN ACTION

"Too often we underestimate the power of a touch, a smile, a kind word, a listening ear, an honest compliment, or the smallest act of caring, all of which have the potential to turn a life around."

–Leo Buscaglia

The Adventure

Your heart is a muscle in more ways than one. Commit thirty small acts of love over thirty days and watch your heart and soul expand. Guaranteed, you'll experience a profound shift in how easily it becomes to share love after these beguilingly simple actions. This first book in the Adventures in Compassion Series is an adventure in generously sharing yourself and your love with others.

How hard can it be to smile at five people? What's the big deal in sending a thank-you note? It's not the individual acts of love that makes the month an inspirational and fun challenge. It's the commitment you make to mindfully share yourself. This is an opportunity to bring more love, joy and compassion to your friends, family and community.

No special equipment is required. Except for the days you give away a dollar, share food or give-away a favorite book, it won't tax your material resources, either. What it will cost is stepping outside your comfort zone once or twice. Don't be surprised if the universe conspires to have a particular day's act of love happen in the absolute craziest of circumstances. On other days, the universe may conspire to turn something you thought would be an outrageous challenge into an action as effortless as breathing.

Every player reaps the reward of increased compassion. Those around you experience more love. Use the book as a guide to an adventure in loving and you'll discover its power to touch, heal and inspire. If you've never paid attention before, you'll also discover your favorite ways to love others as well as those which take a little more effort.

Why 30 Days?

When was the last time you did anything for thirty days straight? It's not easy. The only thing gyms can count on slimming down in January is gym attendance come January 30th. The ones still there are the ones who get results.

You don't have to do all thirty days. Nope. Even if you only do the exercises for a week or two, you'll benefit. But like anything, if you are interested in making a positive change in your life, it takes an investment—time and discipline.

Try it out for seven days. The worst that can happen is a few extra smiles in the world. However, I guaranteed that if you play full out and commit to the thirty days, you will experience a profound sense of love, connection and expansion of personal power. Yes, I said, guaranteed. By the way, gyms can guarantee weight loss if you commit to working out three times a week and watching what you eat. So, yes, I guarantee a profound shift IF you commit to the adventure.

A handful of readers turned adventurers will earn the lofty title "Grandmaster of Compassion" by completing each day's challenge without skipping a beat. To those of you who complete all thirty actions on the very first go-round, Kudos!

Neither titles nor heightened self-esteem are the true prizes, of course. The true prize is rediscovering your friends, your family and your world. In other words, rediscovering you!

Loving is an art. Mastery requires practice. Jump in. Start committing small acts of love. The key is staying in the game. Take advantage of the Keeping Score questions to nurture inspiration. Your answers will help guide the final acts of love.

Like all love, this game is more fun when shared. Invite friends, family, coworkers, church members, book club, meet-up group, knitting circle or neighbors to propel you forward with a little friendly competition.

Need a fundraiser?
Get all the members in your group, charity, church or workplace to accept pledges from friends, family and coworkers for each day's action. Try 10cents/day or $1 for each day's act of love. That will net $3 or $30 per pledge at month's end. Have some fun, spread some love and raise some cash for a good cause.

Is there such a thing as too much love in the world?

We make it just to give it away. And in giving it away, more flows back to us from directions we never imagined. Creating love in the ordinary moments of life increases our capacity to generate it, to gift it to others and to hold it within our own being. Love is the foundation of compassionate action.

Love appears wherever and whenever we give it a space to show up, and stays as long as we court its presence. It's energy. It's light. It's not a feeling. It's doesn't dwell in a fixed state. It can't be copyrighted, patented, re-engineered, rationed, bottled or monopolized. It flows out of us and into us. The more love we make and give away, the more light we have for ourselves.

"All you need is love."
–*John Lennon*

Day 1: Smile

> *"Every time you smile at someone, it is an action of love, a gift to that person, a beautiful thing."*
> — Mother Teresa

Today's Adventure

Share your smile with five people you normally might not.

Compassion in Action

Without realizing it, most of us develop smile guidelines. We smile at people we know. We smile at people who are "safe". We smile in pleasant public situations. We smile when we think it will get us better service. And, certainly, when it might yield a discount or benefit. On the other side, we don't smile at people in certain occupations. We don't smile at people of a certain class. We don't smile at people of a certain age.

My guess is we're afraid that the smile may turn into a hello and then a conversation. Afraid of the unknown, we let fear prevent us from lighting up each other's day.

Smiling at your parents, kids or the coworkers you hang out with regularly is not the type of stretch that makes this an adventure. This is day one of committing small acts of love and kindness. As you go through the day, notice your smile guidelines. Then go beyond them. Smile.

Mastering Compassion

Every time you think about smiling at someone and hear that little voice give you a reason not to do it, do it anyway.

Keeping Score

Did you complete today's action?

If you did, describe what happened.

What was it like for you? If you did not complete it, what got in the way?

> *"A smile is a curve that sets everything straight."*
> –Phyllis Diller

Day 2: Compliment Someone You Know

"A compliment is something like a kiss through a veil."
−Victor Hugo

Today's Adventure

Compliment someone you know in a way that conveys your love, respect or admiration.

Compassion in Action

Speaking the compliment is the second part of today's challenge. The first part is taking a moment to conscientiously discover what you love and enjoy about the people in your life. It may be what they do, how they do it or a way that they are with others. It's entirely permissible to think about possible compliments before you speak. You can even think them over before you leave the house if that makes it any easier.

Think of three to five people you'll definitely see later today. What can you compliment them on based on what you already know about them? How can you say it in a way that helps them see who they are, what they do or how they do it as a gift? Whether you speak complimentary words to these individuals or others, you'll make their day.

"Nice shoes!" is a compliment. So is, "You always wear really nice shoes." But a soul validating version is to say "I've never met anyone who can pull together a beautiful ensemble as seemingly effortless as you. There is a talented artist inside you that shows up in the way you dress." Now, that's creating the experience of love with words.

Mastering Compassion

Compliment someone who normally irritates or annoys you. If you don't experience anyone as irritating or annoying, compliment someone you come across whom you find unappealing in even the slightest way for any reason.

Keeping Score

Who did you compliment?

What was the compliment?

If you did not compliment anyone, what got in the way?

> *"I can live for two months on a good compliment."*
> *—Mark Twain*

Day 3 Smell The Flowers, Notice the Birds

"You're only here for a short visit. Don't hurry, don't worry. And be sure to smell the flowers along the way."
–Walter Hagen

Today's Adventure

Stop and smell the flowers or notice the birds and bees.

Compassion in Action

Graciously accepting a gift is as loving as giving one. Every day Mother Nature greets us with gifts. The sights, sounds and fragrances of nature are gifts we learn to ignore or take for granted. Today's act of love is to graciously receive one of Mother Nature's precious gifts—her flowers, her creatures or scenes.

Take a deep inhale of a fragrant flower. Doing it in view of others may inspire someone else to stop and smell the flowers, too. It's as contagious as yawning. Make time to truly marvel at a sunset. Steal away into nature and listen to the birds and bees.

Compassion for our planet is the first step in caring for her properly.

Mastering Compassion

Pick or purchase a flower to place in your hair, your lapel or to sit on a desk or table. It doesn't have to be fancy or expensive. If you choose to pick one instead of purchasing, make sure it is taken from an open field or public area. An act of love never involves theft or trespassing.

Keeping Score

What aspect of Mother Nature did you appreciate?

How?

If you did not complete it, what got in the way?

> *"I think it pisses God off if you walk by the color purple in a field somewhere and don't notice it."*
> *—Alice Walker*

Day 4 "You're Beautiful"

> *"Beauty is eternity gazing at itself in a mirror."*
> –Khalil Gibran

Today's Adventure

Tell someone that they are beautiful.

Compassion in Action

Beauty and attractiveness are sometimes found together, but not always. Beauty is in the eye of the beholder. No need to scour the people you come across to find a person worthy of being told they are beautiful. It can be found in every single person you come across when you focus your eyes to perceive it. The more you practice recognizing the beauty in others, the easier it is to recognize your own true beauty.

Beauty resides in eyes trained by love to seek it out. When we see one to another's beauty, we glimpse one to another's heart.

Mastering Compassion

In the course of the day, notice whom you categorize as less than attractive. Practice looking at them in search of their deeper beauty.

Keeping Score

Whose beauty did you acknowledge and how did you say it?

What was it like for you?

If you did not complete it, what got in the way?

> *"Life is full of beauty. Notice it. Notice the bumble bee, the small child, and the smiling faces. Smell the rain, and feel the wind. Live your life to the fullest potential, and fight for your dreams."*
> *—Ashley Smith*

Day 5 Listen

"I like to listen. I have learned a great deal from listening carefully. Most people never listen."
–Ernest Hemingway

Today's Adventure

Listen to someone.

Compassion in Action

Anyone who offers their ear without adding the lips is extending compassion. Something incredible happens when we are truly heard. We may not say anything, but we know the difference between being listened to and being humored or tolerated.

Someone says, "Can I talk to you? There's something on my mind." The other person says, "Yeah, sure." Oftentimes, sooner than later, the listener becomes the talker. Unsolicited advice flows freely. Empathetic stories creep in and then take over the conversation. Even when the listener does not advise or share their similar tales, judgments on the legitimacy of the speaker's concern dictates the response. Listening is an act of discipline. Far from passive, the silence of listening is a miraculous act of love.

We're powerful beings. Smart, too. When we speak our concerns aloud, we hear ourselves. Our frustration dissipates. Our options become apparent. We solve our own problems when we can see them. Somehow, seeing through someone else's ears adds clarity.

Mastering Compassion

Call someone with whom you can predict every miserable, predictable turn in the conversation. And instead of saying the usual responses, just listen. If you usually give advice, don't. If in the past you've tried to explain something to them, just for today, fuhgettaboutit. Grant them fresh ears.

Keeping Score

To whom did you listen today?

If you did not listen to someone, what got in the way?

"One of the most sincere forms of respect is actually listening to what another has to say."
–Bryant H. McGill

Day 6 Clean Something

"Find your place on the planet. Dig in, and take responsibility from there."
–Gary Snyder

Today's Adventure

Clean something that doesn't belong to you.

Compassion in Action

Pick up a single piece of trash off the street. Clean something at your place of work that it is not your job to clean. Wipe down the counter in a public restroom. Of course, only do this if it does not cause you to violate anyone else's sense of privacy and personal space. Definitely, only do so if it will not break any laws or established rules. Notice any resistance to cleaning up other people's messes.

It may not be your mess, but it is your environment. Whose world is it, if it isn't yours?

Mastering Compassion

As you go through your day, notice any litter on the sidewalk, around trash cans, in parks, etc. Pick up five pieces of litter, trash, recyclables or other disposed items. Do this in addition to cleaning something that doesn't belong to you.

Keeping Score

Where and what did you clean?

If you did not complete today's act of compassion, what got in the way?

*"Everybody wants to save the Earth;
nobody wants to help Mom do the dishes."*
–P.J. O'Rourke

Day 7 Planet Earth

"We should honor Mother Earth with gratitude; otherwise our spirituality may become hypocritical."
−Radhanath Swami

Today's Adventure

Pray for the planet.

Compassion in Action

If you don't believe in prayer, imagine the world surrounded by love or light. Do this for ten minutes. Ten minutes can seem longer than you think, so consider breaking it up into plants, animals, marine life, people, mountains, weather, global warming phenomena, etc.

If neither prayer nor imagining do it for you, then learn one new way you can live harmoniously on the planet. Then do it.

Mastering Compassion

Find one thing you can start doing for the health of our planet and begin doing it today. If you don't recycle paper, start there. If you don't recycle bottles and cans, that's also a good one. If you buy bottled water by the case, invest in a refillable water bottle and fill with filtered water from home. Replace thirsty plants with others that require the least water possible in your climate. These are just a few ideas.

Keeping Score

Which way did you choose to honor the planet?

Is this something you can do regularly?

If you did not complete it, what got in the way?

> *"You carry Mother Earth within you. She is not outside of you. Mother Earth is not just your environment. In that insight of inter-being, it is possible to have real communication with the Earth, which is the highest form of prayer."*
> *—Thich Nhat Hanh*

Day 8 Give Away One Dollar

"I have tried to teach people there are three kicks in every dollar: one, when you make it; two, when you have it. The third kick is when you give it away—and it is the biggest kick of all." –William Allen White

Today's Adventure

Give away a dollar.

Compassion in Action

It's up to you whether you choose someone who is requesting money or to do so on a whim. If you live or work in an area populated with panhandlers or representatives of charities requesting donations at places of business, this will be a little easier to do. To count, you have to actually hand the person your dollar, getting nothing in return. No chocolate bars, no extra foam on your latte. Notice the number of people you come across in a day who could use your dollar.

This isn't about the amount of money you give. If you're tempted to make it five or ten or one hundred dollars, that's something different. You can do that, too. But on one occasion give away exactly one dollar and notice how many people you come across in a day that can use a single dollar. If you're rich, it's humbling. If you're struggling, it's still humbling.

If you have any concern that giving away money devalues the receiver or the possibility that your dollar will support a poor life choice, let it go. Complete the day's act of love and leave the rest to a higher power to manage.

Mastering Compassion

Go online and give ten minutes to donate sponsors money to those in need at no cost to you. FreeRice.com donates free rice to the hungry in rich and poor nations. For each correct answer to vocabulary, math, geography, science or a few other subjects, they donate ten grains of rice. Ten minutes could result in a donation of a cup of rice. That won't end hunger, but it does help you appreciate that our many ways to help those in need besides writing a check from your own account. Other websites that contribute someone else's resources to good causes are Charitii.org, thenoprofits.com and care2.org.

Keeping Score

To whom did you give your dollar?

Why that person?

What did you notice about the level of basic or financial need in your community?

If you did not complete it, what got in the way?

"*Every dollar that is printed should not represent a debt to private bankers. It should represent an investment potential in the common good, in the common needs of our country.*" –Cynthia McKinney

Day 9   Express Thanks

"Thank you is the best prayer that anyone could say. I say that one a lot. Thank you expresses extreme gratitude, humility, understanding." –Alice Walker

Today's Adventure

Write a thank you note and actually send it.

Compassion in Action

It doesn't matter for what. It can be for something recent or something someone did long ago. Don't worry about how much time has passed. Thank you notes are never too late. Don't worry about sloppy handwriting, poor grammar, your style, or the format you choose. Only think about the value of letting someone know the difference they made.

Mastering Compassion

Send two.

Keeping Score

Who did you thank?

What was it like for you?

If you did not complete it, what got in the way?

> *"Let us be grateful to the people who make us happy; they are the charming gardeners who make our souls blossom."*
> *—Marcel Proust*

DAY 10   COMPLIMENT A STRANGER

"Everybody likes a compliment."
–Abraham Lincoln

Today's Adventure

Compliment a stranger.

Compassion in Action

Just like Day 2's compliment of someone you knew, say it in a way that helps them see who they are, what they do or how they do it as a gift? If you are someone who does this easily, compliment five strangers. There's a great blog entry on complimenting a stranger at <u>Live Simply by Annie</u>.

Mastering Compassion

As you go throughout your day, notice the times you consider smiling at someone and choose not to do so. Ask yourself what it was about them that turned you off. Or, said a different way, what was your thought about them that took away your willingness to smile at will?

Keeping Score

Who did you compliment?

What was about them that inspired you to compliment them as opposed to all the other people you could have complimented?

Which compliment do you hear the most?

Which compliments are you most likely to give?

If you did not complete it, what got in the way?

"The fragrance of flowers spreads only in the direction of the wind. But the goodness of a person spreads in all directions."
–Chanakya

Day 11 Give Away Words

*"The things I want to know are in books;
my best friend is the man who'll get me a
book I ain't read."*
–Abraham Lincoln

Today's Adventure

Give away a book.

Compassion in Action

Choose a book that really made a difference in your life. The real gift isn't the book. It's the time you'll take thinking about who among your friends, family or acquaintances might truly appreciate it. If, after thinking of everyone you know, you can't imagine a single person who'd be interested, then drop it off at a school, shelter or used bookstore with a wish that it lands in the right person's hands. If you don't have any books to share, substitute a different artistic expression that has inspired you. A unique compilation of music on CD might work.

Although it will be awesome if the person actually reads the book, plays the music or otherwise enjoys your gift, that's not your concern today. We make love to give it away. If they read it, play it or enjoy it and tell you about it, then that is their gift of love to you.

Separate giving from your expectations of how it ought to be received or used.

Mastering Compassion

Find one other item of any type to give away. It can be another book or CD. Or, something else that its recipient will be able to use, appreciate or enjoy.

Keeping Score

Which book, CD or other item did you give away?

Why did you choose that item?

What is it you hope the gift provides the recipient?

If you did not complete today's act of love, what got in the way?

> *"Books are a uniquely portable magic."*
> –Stephen King

Day 12 Share A Talent

"All labor that uplifts humanity has dignity and importance and should be undertaken with painstaking excellence."
–Martin Luther King, Jr.

Today's Adventure

Share one of your talents.

Compassion in Action

This can look about seven and half billion different ways. If you're a musician, surprise someone with a song. Do you cook? Make a special meal for a friend, a shut-in, a neighbor, a colleague or a whole group of folks. Not an artsy person? Mr. Fixit, fix something. Ms. Organized, organize something for someone.

It's up to you how much time you dedicate to completing today's act of love. All of us have multiple gifts. Choose to share the one that your day's schedule allows you to share comfortably to keep the spirit of fun and ease in the game. However, if you can go all out, don't hold back.

If you're at a complete loss, scroll back through numbers 1 through 11 and do the one you enjoyed the most.

Mastering Compassion

Locate a charity that can use your talent and schedule a time to volunteer within the next thirty days.

Keeping Score

Which talent did you share?]

With whom did you share it?

What was it like to share that talent with that person?

If you did not complete today's act of love, what got in the way?

> *"You give but little when you give of your possessions. It is when you give of yourself that you truly give."*
> *—Khalil Gibran*

Day 13 Donate Something

> *"Happiness doesn't result from what we get, but from what we give."*
> –Ben Carson

Today's Adventure

Donate Something.

Compassion in Action

There's something you have and don't want that someone else doesn't have and does want. Even if it's a want they don't yet know they have. There's a thrift store, charity or shelter that will benefit from your donation.

If there's something in your closet that looks practically new but you haven't worn it or used in over a year, there's a good chance it's time has passed for you. If you haven't used or worn it in three years and it still looks good…give it away and clear a space for something new to come to you.

Mastering Compassion

Most of us have more than a single item that is sitting in the house unused and unlikely to ever be used. If you can spare a few extra minutes to donate several items that another can use.

Keeping Score

What did you give away and to whom?

For how long had you considered giving this item away, if this applies?

How did it feel to donate that item or give it away?

If you did not complete today's act of love, what got in the way?

> *"If you're in the luckiest one percent of humanity, you owe it to the rest of humanity to think about the other 99 percent."*
> *–Warren Buffett*

Day 14 Express Gratitude

"True happiness is to enjoy the present, without anxious dependence upon the future, not to amuse ourselves with either hopes or fears but to rest satisfied with what we have, which is sufficient, for he that is so wants nothing. The greatest blessings of mankind are within us and within our reach. A wise man is content with his lot, whatever it may be, without asking for what he has not."
–Lucius Annaeus Seneca

Today's Adventure

Express your gratitude.

Compassion in Action

Think of five things you're glad you have and tell someone about it. Whether you have tons of material possessions or a handful, there is so much to be grateful for on any given day. If you're reading this, you are still alive. Today is an opportunity. Two things to be grateful for before we even get to stuff. Are there people in your life that make a difference? Which talents, gifts, abilities or experiences add value to your life?

Mastering Compassion

Tell five different people five things you're grateful for without telling them it is a part of this assignment. Notice what it inspires in them.

Keeping Score

What are five to ten things you are grateful for today?

What was it like to share your gratitude with others?

How did they respond?

If you did not complete today's act of love, what got in the way?

> *"When you practice gratefulness, there is a sense of respect toward others."*
> –Dalai Lama

Day 15 Use Words Intentionally

"Listen to many. Speak to a few."
—William Shakespeare

Today's Adventure

Pay attention to how you use our greatest technology, words. Use words intentionally.

Compassion in Action

Our words can create love in an instant. They can also create upset and dis-ease. When you recognize the power of your speaking, moment-by-moment, you begin to recognize how much your words create your experience of the world. How often do you talk about problems, worries or other people as problems? How often do you repeat meaningless phrases or cliché phrases in place of an authentic conversation?

Avoid asking superfluous questions. Only ask how someone is doing if you intend to listen attentively to their response. Avoid using offensive words.

Minding your words is an act of love toward everyone you are around today.

Mastering Compassion

In addition to the above, refrain from sarcasm, teasing and gossip throughout the day.

Keeping Score

Was any part of speaking intentionally harder for you than another?

How was your day different from most other days?

If you did not complete today's act of love, what got in the way?

> *"Somewhere we know that without silence words lose their meaning, that without listening, speaking no longer heals, that without distance closeness cannot cure."*
> –Henri Nouwen

Day 16 Love You

"To love yourself right now, just as you are, is to give yourself heaven. Don't wait until you die. If you wait, you die now. If you love, you live now."
–Alan Cohen

Today's Adventure

Do something just for you.

Compassion in Action

You're doing great! You're halfway through 30 days of love. Treat yourself. Preferably, to something free. This is a gift of time.

Watch a sunset. Listen to your favorite music. Take a stroll. Write in your journal. Write yourself a letter of appreciation or congratulation. Take a nap. Indulge in a bubble bath. There's something special about you. There's a reason you exist. A difference you make being the unique combination of traits that you are.

It is definitely more difficult to be compassionate with others if we neglect compassionate action toward ourselves. If you never feel worthy of a break, how can you cut someone else a break?

Take responsibility for your own daily joy. That act affirms to yourself and the universe that you know your unique value.

Mastering Compassion

Do something for yourself today that you've been putting off, avoiding or waiting to find the time. Don't settle. How can you value the dreams and desires of others, if you deny the value of your own?

Keeping Score

What did you do just for you today?

What was it like for you?

If you did not complete today's act of love, what got in the way?

> *"Love is like a beautiful flower which I may not touch, but whose fragrance makes the garden a place of delight just the same."*
> –Helen Keller

Day 17   Love Through Style

"I really don't know how to be anyone else, and whenever I try to be anyone else, I fail miserably. Or I disappoint myself. It doesn't build my self-esteem, and it doesn't help me grow me at all."
–Queen Latifah

Today's Adventure

Love yourself. Love your style.

Compassion in Action

This is the day you go out looking your very best. Whether it's Monday or Sunday, go out in style. Your style! Done right! Attend to the extras; wear the item that looks really great on you, without needing an excuse or an event to share how good it looks on you. This isn't about you. You're sharing love with the world. When you look great, you have a completely different experience. And so does everyone around you.

Mastering Compassion

Look for the individuals who wear their style and wear it well. Notice what you think of them. Tell at least one of these self-styled individuals how much you appreciate their style.

Keeping Score

What did you wear today or how did you share your style?

What was it like for you?

If you did not complete today's act of love, what got in the way?

> *"It takes generosity to discover the whole through others. If you realize you are only a violin, you can open yourself up to the world by playing your role in the concert."*
> –Jacques Yves Cousteau

Day 18   Give 10 Minutes

"Service to others is the rent you pay for your room here on earth."
—Muhammad Ali

Today's Adventure

Give away 10 minutes of your time.

Compassion in Action

There are lots of options with this one. Whether you have a busy schedule from daybreak to bedtime or stroll through your day with little on your calendar, the conscious act of giving 10 minutes to someone or something else is definitely an act of love. Ask someone how they're doing and do so with genuine curiosity. Look around and notice if there's someone at work, in your home or on the street who could use a helping hand to finish something, start something or move something. Don't be shy. And don't worry about starting something you can't finish. Choose something in which ten minutes will make a difference, big or small.

Mastering Compassion

Find a way to give a full thirty minutes to someone else. Help them with a project that is important to them. If there is no one around you working on any type of project at home, work, church or play, you'll need to be creative. Is there a business establishment or local not-for-profit organization that you've thought of offering to help in some way? Today's the day.

Keeping Score

What did you do and for whom?

How did the person respond?

If you did not complete today's act of love, what got in the way?

> *"My religion is very simple. My religion is kindness."*
> –Dalai Lama

Day 19 Say "I Love You."

"Love makes your soul crawl out from its hiding place."
–Zora Neale Hurston

Today's Adventure

Say "I love you" to someone you normally do not.

Compassion in Action

This might be your significant other or a parent or a sibling. It could be a close friend. If "I love you" flows off your lips like a river to the sea, it may take a few moments to think of someone whom you do love but to whom you do not express it aloud in three simple words.

Mastering Compassion

In addition to telling the person "I love you," include the details of what it is about them that inspires in you the awareness of valuing their unique contribution your life and the world.

Keeping Score

To whom did you say "I love you"?

Search your relationships. Name three people who don't hear "I love you" very often.

If you did not complete today's act of love, what got in the way?

> *"Love is that condition in the human spirit so profound that it allows me to survive, and better than that, to thrive with passion, compassion and style."*
> —Maya Angelou

Day 20 Make A List of Loves

"The soul is not where it lives but where it loves."
—Thomas Fuller

Today's Adventure

Write out the names of 20 people you love and another 20 names of people who love you.

Compassion in Action

Depending on your life circumstances, a list of twenty people who love you either sounds super short or ridiculously long. Now that we're twenty days into the game, you recognize that love comes in myriad forms. Define love broadly and become present to the sea of love that surrounds you.

Mastering Compassion

Pick at least three of the names on the list of those you love and tell them "I love you." Like yesterday, no variations on those three words, but feel free to add more words before or after as you like.

Keeping Score

Did you find this exercise easier or harder than expected?

Did anything surprise you as you completed them?

If you did not complete today's act of love, what got in the way?

> *"Just as there is no loss of basic energy in the universe, so no thought or action is without its effects, present or ultimate, seen or unseen, felt or unfelt."*
> *—Norman Cousins.*

Day 21 Share Food

"If you really want to make a friend, go to someone's house and eat with him...the people who give you their food give you their heart."
—Cesar Chavez

Today's Adventure

Share food.

Compassion in Action

This act of love separates the haves from the have nots. You either have a love of cooking and eating or you don't.

If you are a have, this is a day to cook, bake or buy a dish or a delight for someone else to consume and enjoy. Chefs and wannabe chefs might make a meal for friends or family. If you cook the meals in your home each day, make today's meal something new, something loved or something comforting.

If you're a have not as in 'have not a bit of interest' in baking or cooking or selecting especially delectable food stuff for another, there are other ways to share food.

>   *Donate food to a local food pantry. Canned goods, cereals, rice and other staples are almost always a good bet. If

you're short on funds, share from your own cabinets.

*Find a location that serves meals and help out. The opportunity to serve food may be granted to a regular cadre of volunteers.

Mastering Compassion

Provide a meal for someone. Churches and charities offer meals to those who are shut-in, disabled or going through economic uncertainty. If you know someone in this situation, share a plate of something you've prepared if it will be accepted and appreciated. Another option is a gift card to a local grocery store or restaurant. I'm not a fan of the fast food diet, but a $5 gift card to a place with a dollar menu buys a meal. A donation to one of the churches or charities that provide meals is another great option.

Keeping Score

What did you share and with whom?

What was it like for you?

If you did not complete today's act of love, what got in the way?

"Sharing food with another human being is an intimate act that should not be indulged in lightly."
—*M. F. K. Fisher*

Day 22 Touch of Love

> *"Nothing is so healing as the human touch."*
> –Bobby Fischer

Today's Adventure

Touch a loved one today. (You know what I mean.)

Compassion in Action

If you are not a hugger or hugging is not part of your relationship with a parent, sibling or friend, today's the day to hug. Holding hands works, too.

While walking my dog in the park, I saw two young girls, probably seven- or eight-years-old. They skipped across the grass holding hands en route to the play area. It stood out to me. In American society, we don't expect to see friends holding hands. Even couples sometimes limit holding hands to date nights.

We are physical beings. Physical touch has the capacity to heal. When a parent kisses their child's "boo-boo" it is helping the healing process. Search the web and you will find that many a study has confirmed that touch is powerful medicine.

- Put your arm around a loved one's shoulder.
- Hug a parent, child, spouse, friend or relative.

- Pat a close friend, relative or coworker on the back for a job well done or in gratitude.
- Hold hands while you walk with friend, child, spouse or relative.

If you'll only see coworkers and acquaintances today, weigh whether a pat on the back for a job well done is an appropriate option. If not, hug a tree, lie in the grass or roll around in the snow. Find a way to connect physically with your environment if there is absolutely no way for you to appropriately connect with another person.

Mastering Compassion

As you go through the day, notice if you see any individuals who may not enjoy the luxury of human touch on a daily basis. It is enough just to engage in noticing. If you are especially empathetic, this exercise may be emotionally taxing. Only if you are moved to do so, ask one of them if you can offer them a hug.

Keeping Score

Describe today's act of love?

If you did not complete today's act of love, what got in the way?

> *"A bell's not a bell 'til you ring it. A song's not a song 'til you sing it. Love in your heart wasn't put there to stay. Love isn't love 'til you give it away!"*
> –Oscar Hammerstein II

Day 23 Do Something For The Planet

"The earth we share is not just a rock tossed through space, but a living, nurturing being. She cares for us. She deserves our care in return."
—Michael Jackson

Today's Adventure

Do something for the planet.

Compassion in Action

Recycle something you normally do not. If you're not an avid recycler, this will be easy. Instead of putting that bottle, can or paper in the trash, find a place to recycle it. If you have an old phone or other electronic device, use the internet to find a nearby drop-off location.

Composting trash will grow your garden greener. Prefer cash? Give $5 to a charity that plants trees, conserves nature or protects habitats and species. The Canopy Project is part of The Earth Day Network and highly recommended. It may not be your mess, but it is your environment.

Looking for something you can do from your computer or mobile device? Replace your current search browser with http://ecosearch.org, http://searchkindly.org or http://goodsearch.com to donate to charities each time you search. Your searches will help save the planet. Also, check out http://ecologyfund.com. You click and sponsors donate to earth-preserving charities. Also, coming in mid-September, Make A Difference Every Day.

Mastering Compassion

Discover and take on one new habit that supports the earth.

Keeping Score

What did you do for planet earth today?

If you did not complete today's act of love, what got in the way?

> *"We won't have a society if we destroy the environment."*
> –Margaret Mead

Day 24 Make A Request

"There are times we are givers, but other times we have to let others give to us."
–Paul Hoffman

Today's Adventure

Ask someone for something.

Compassion in Action

Give the gift of contribution. Let someone do something for you. Almost all of us know someone who loves to do stuff for us. Trouble is we don't always want what they wish to contribute to us. It may be a child who wants to fix-up our hair, but we're too busy. Ask them for a makeover. If your spouse makes too much of a mess when they do that thing they love to do for you, ask them to do it for you.

And, of course, thank them afterwards.

Mastering Compassion

Ask a relative to do something for you. Your mother would love this one. If there's a relative that is always asking you for a favor, ask them for something that it is within their power to do for you.

Keeping Score

Whom did you allow to contribute to you and in what way?

How did they respond to your request?

If you did not complete today's act of love, what got in the way?

> *"To solve any problem, here are three*
> *questions to ask yourself: First, what*
> *could I do? Second, what could I read?*
> *And third, who could I ask?"*
> *–Jim Rohn*

Day 25 Share Laughter

"Like a welcome summer rain, humor may suddenly cleanse and cool the earth, the air and you."
–Langston Hughes

Today's Adventure

Make someone laugh.

Compassion in Action

Laughter heals. It releases pent up, stale energy. That makes laughter an act of compassion.

Know a good joke? Know a bad one? Ever notice that the silliest jokes sometimes get the biggest laughs. Jokes told incorrectly can work too. A woman at work who was nearing retirement started telling joke about the three good things that come from having Alzheimer's. She stated the first two and when she got to the third, stumbled a bit and finally said, "Oh darn, I can't remember the last one." We all laughed. Turned out there was a real third benefit that completed the joke, but her new version is the joke we retell.

If jokes aren't your thing, try a funny face. Kids love them. Young kids love them. Those going through the teenage years are more likely to scowl at a funny face than laugh.

Costumes, funny hats or a YouTube comedy scene shared, all work.

Mastering Compassion

Surf the web and find a new joke to make your own. Share it more than once.

Keeping Score

Who did you make laugh and how?

How much fun did you have with today's small act of love?

If you did not complete today's act of love, what got in the way?

"A good laugh heals a lot of hurts."
–Madeleine L'Engle

Day 26 Forgive

"To forgive is to set a prisoner free and discover that the prisoner was you."
–Lewis Smedes

Today's Adventure

Forgive someone.

Compassion in Action

If forgiveness were easy, there wouldn't be enough books written on it to fill a small bookstore. Religions, twelve step programs and healing arts all acknowledge the power of forgiveness to transform our life. If you're ready to forgive big, do it. Otherwise, we can keep it simple.

Think of an action someone took that still bothers you to do this day—a remark, an omission, an inconsideration. Now, here's the shortcut to accessing the spirit of forgiveness. Think of a time when you did something similar to someone else, intentionally or not. Take a moment to look carefully until you find something relatable. Why did you do it? How did it affect the other person? What would life be like if everyone who met you was told that story about you and nothing else? Extending forgiveness expands the heart.

Mastering Compassion

If you haven't apologized for a grievance someone holds against you, do that today also. If there is no way to reach this person because they are no longer living or relocated to someplace unknown to you, apologize aloud as if they can hear you or write it out in a letter. If you write the letter, I recommend destroying it afterward as an act of accepting your own forgiveness by letting it go.

Keeping Score

Whom did you forgive today and for what past act?

How did you feel afterwords*?

If you did not complete today's act of love, what got in the way?

> "Forgiveness is not always easy. At times, it feels more painful than the wound we suffered, to forgive the one that inflicted it. And yet, there is no peace without forgiveness."
> —Marianne Williamson

*term courtesy of GilbertMarina

Day 27 Give Something Away

> *"Every gift from a friend is a wish for your happiness."*
> –Richard Bach

Today's Adventure

Give something away.

Compassion in Action

There's something you have and don't want that someone else doesn't have and does want. Even if it's a want they don't yet know they have.

Before you search for the nearest thrift store, take a moment to find out if you have something to offer someone you know.

> *Examples:*
> **A friend complimented you on a scarf that you don't often wear. Gift it to her.*
> **A child loves to play with something of yours that is collecting dust except for when he plays with it. Assuming it isn't a safety hazard for the child's age, gift it.*
> **A coworker loves a desktop knick-knack that isn't particularly sentimental to you. Gift it. Casually.*

A neighbor constantly comments about a garden decoration. Gift it.

If it is too awkward for you to give it away today or impossible because you won't see the people who come to mind, then, by all means, drop something off at a local thrift store, shelter or other appropriate location.

Tip: If there's something in your closet that looks practically new but you haven't worn it or used in over a year, there's a good chance it's time has passed for you. If you haven't used or worn it in three years and it still looks good…give it away and clear a space for something new to come to you.

Mastering Compassion

Give away something that you've been holding onto for all the wrong reasons. Is there something left over from a long ago relationship that is anchoring you to the past? Is there an item you've outgrown, but you are hanging onto it as a symbol of glory days gone by? Put the past where it belongs and seek out today's gift, today's love, today's glory.

Keeping Score

What did you give away?

What was it like for you?

If you did not complete today's act of love, what got in the way?

"For it is in giving that we receive."
—*St. Francis of Assisi*

Day 28 Be Curious

"Some say we are responsible for those we love. Others know we are responsible for those who love us."
—Nikki Giovanni

Today's Adventure

Ask someone you love what they'd most like to receive from you.

Compassion in Action

The gift you are giving them is being curious about what matters to them. If it is also something you can do, then by all means do it. Again, the gift is hearing what matters to them. Hear it. Receive it. To know them is to love them.

The Five Love Languages by Gary Chapman explores and categories the different ways we give and receive love. His list: Words of Affirmation; Gifts; Acts of Service; Quality Time; and Physical Touch.

Some of the frustration we feel in relationships occurs when mismatched love languages interfere with the successful communication of the love we feel with another. If your loved one prefers words of affirmation, while you are spending money showering them with gifts, the experience of love is present, but may not be as satisfying. Imagine asking, "What would you most like to receive from me?" You might discover that something that would never occur to you as special or important is something your partner, child or parent has been waiting to see, know, hear, receive or experience.

Today is an opportunity to get to know the person you ask. Be prepared for the possibility that you what they want is not something you are prepared to offer or complete. That's OK. Don't believe me?

Ask yourself when someone you loved asked you what you most wanted to receive from them. It moves us. If it never happens, we wish it had. Just once.

Mastering Compassion

If you cannot give them what they'd most like to receive from you today, figure out when you can do so and then do it.

Keeping Score

Who did you ask?

What did they say?

If you did not complete today's act of love, what got in the way?

> *"You are beginning to see that any man to whom you can do favor is your friend, and that you can do a favor to almost anyone."*
> *—Mark Caine*

Day 29 Love Again

"We are what we repeatedly do. Excellence, then, is not an act, but a habit."
—William Durant

Today's Adventure

Repeat whichever act of love was the hardest this month.

Compassion in Action

Which day was the hardest to complete? Do that one again and see if it is any easier. Notice how your interactions with others have changed over the last month.

If you have completed the prior twenty-eight exercises each day, you have experienced the magic of an expanding heart. Your view of what it means to be a compassionate, loving being has altered powerfully and permanently. No doubt, if you play this game again, it will be a grander adventure than you can imagine.

Just in case you found completing the game once was enough, today is the day you find out how much your heart has grown. The question "What got in your way" at the end of each day provided an opportunity to notice which actions were more challenging. Having trouble picking a do-over day? Use the answers to the question "What got in the way"

Mastering Compassion

Double up on the repeat. Compliment two strangers instead of one. Donate two things instead of one. Give 20 minutes instead of 10. You get the idea.

Keeping Score

Which day did you repeat?

What was different this time around?

If you did not complete today's act of love, what got in the way?

> *"I've missed more than 9000 shots in my career. I've lost almost 300 games. 26 times, I've been trusted to take the game winning shot and missed. I've failed over and over and over again in my life. And that is why I succeed."*
> *—Michael Jordan*

DAY 30   REPEAT YOUR FAVORITE

"Today is life—the only life you are sure of. Make the most of today. Get interested in something. Shake yourself awake. Develop a hobby. Let the winds of enthusiasm sweep through you. Live today with gusto."
–Dale Carnegie

Today's Adventure

Pick your favorite day. Now go big!

Compassion in Action

Adventures in Compassion completes today. You've reached your destination. If you've successfully completed each day's act of love, you are a master at compassion. Today is the day to show off.

Pretend that a chorus of angels has been watching you throughout the month. Sometimes they helped, sometimes they challenged you. Now they applaud your arrival at Day 30.

What is your encore? Somewhere along the way, an act of love occurred to you that seemed too ridiculous to tackle. Perhaps today is the day to put all concern aside and go for it.

If nothing else comes to mind, share yourself. Tell someone about the last thirty days' adventures. Share a story of a particular day's love and surprise. Share what was harder than you expected about making love every day. Share what was easier than you anticipated. Share why you chose to challenge yourself in the first place.

Mastering Compassion

Share the impact of completing the Adventures in Compassion with five people you care about. Recommend they grow their heart and soul in the same way you have. Encourage them to have Adventures in Compassion.

Keeping Score

How did you finish off the month?

With which five people did you share your Adventures in Compassion?

If you haven't told them about it, I trust you're not waiting for inspiration to love them with the gift of recommending an Adventure in Compassion.

"There is no passion to be found playing small—in settling for a life that is less than the one you are capable of living."
—Nelson Mandela

Day 31! Congratulations!

"You don't learn to walk by following rules, you learn by doing, and falling over."
–Richard Branson

How do you know if you won?

If you played, you won. You brought a little more sunshine to someone's day. Know that you've added more love to the planet. Every act of love spirals outward touching lives in ways we can't imagine. Just speaking pleasantly to a salesperson who was left upset by a negative interaction before your arrival can change her experience of how the day is going. You walk away, but the good mood spreads from her to the next customer. That customer is then more pleasant to her children and so and so on.

No one playing this game can imagine how many lives they've touched with their love, kindness, generosity and compassion. May the wave of love your actions generate reach the heavens, and may the collective acts of all who play this game harmonize our world.

For those who kept score

Grand Master of Compassion – Complete all 30 acts of love as they were designed each day in the proper order. If you did this on the first go, you are incredible.

You're probably a saint or perhaps an angel walking among the rest of us.

Master of Compassion – Complete each of the 30 tasks. If you completed all 30 acts, but occasionally doubled up after missing a day, you're still a master. "Occasionally" translates to five or fewer missed days.

Compassion Practitioner – Complete at least 25 of the 30 acts of love.

Compassion Apprentice – Complete at least 20 of the 30 acts of love.

Compassion Novice – Complete at least 15 of the 30 acts of love.

Compassion Aspirant – Complete at least 10 of the 30 acts of love.

What's next?

If you are a Grand Master of Compassion, you live and breathe love. You play the game as a matter of living your life. For additional challenge, try the next book in The Compassion Series--Make a Difference Every Day.

For everyone else, you might take a few days to regroup and then start it again. If you didn't do so this time, consider starting on the first day of the next month to make tracking activities easier.

If the novelty of the game has worn off but you enjoyed it all the same, consider adopting your favorite act of love as a daily or weekly habit as appropriate. Or make up your own unique Sunday-to-Saturday seven acts of love weekly combo plan.

Or try one of the other books in The Compassion Series for other Adventures in creating a happier, healthier planet.

My Day 24 Request

Keep love alive. If you think this is worth sharing, please tell others about Make Love Every Day.

Please also take a couple minutes to share your experience with other readers. When you give Adventures In Compassion a five star review, your reach goes beyond your immediate circle of friends, family and acquaintances.

This can be just another cool book of neat actions to take or it can become a movement that transforms the planet. Will you accept my request? It's one more opportunity to do a small act of love and compassion.

> *"Don't cry because it's over, smile because it happened."*
> *–Dr. Seuss*

*"Love is patient,
love is kind.
It does not envy,
it does not boast,
it is not proud.
It does not dishonor others,
it is not self-seeking,
it is not easily angered,
it keeps no record of wrongs.
Love does not delight in evil
but rejoices with the truth.
It always protects,
always trusts,
always hopes,
always perseveres."
1 Corinthians 13:4-7*

Adventures in Compassion is part of The Compassion Series, books designed to o improve the human condition and the world in which we live. Please visit ShyneEveryDay.com. And don't forget to post a review on Amazon.com.

Thank you.

Rahbin Shyne